Guest Book

....

....

....

better notes

© Better Notes · Kochhannstr. 30 · 10249 Berlin · info@betternotes.de · www.betternotes.de
Author & Cover Design: Ilya Malyanov / ilyamalyanov.com

NAME:

....

MESSAGE TO TREASURE:

....
....
....
....
....
....
....
....
....

The most beautiful Photo:

Name:

....

Message to Treasure:

The most beautiful Photo:

Name:

....

Message to Treasure:

....
....
....
....
....
....
....
....
....
....

The most beautiful Photo:

Name:

....

Message to Treasure:

....
....
....
....
....
....
....
....
....

The most beautiful Photo:

NAME:

....

MESSAGE TO TREASURE:

....

....

....

....

....

....

....

....

....

The most beautiful Photo:

Name:

....

Message to Treasure:

....
....
....
....
....
....
....
....
....
....

The most beautiful Photo:

Name:

....

Message to Treasure:

....
....
....
....
....
....
....
....
....
....

The most beautiful Photo:

NAME:

....

MESSAGE TO TREASURE:

....

....

....

....

....

....

....

....

....

....

The most beautiful Photo:

NAME:

....

MESSAGE TO TREASURE:

....
....
....
....
....
....
....
....
....
....

The most beautiful Photo:

NAME:

....

MESSAGE TO TREASURE:

....

....

....

....

....

....

....

....

....

The most beautiful Photo:

Name:

....

Message to Treasure:

....
....
....
....
....
....
....
....
....

The most beautiful Photo:

NAME:

....

MESSAGE TO TREASURE:

....
....
....
....
....
....
....
....
....

The most beautiful Photo:

Name:

....

Message to Treasure:

....
....
....
....
....
....
....
....
....

The most beautiful Photo:

Name:

....

Message to Treasure:

....
....
....
....
....
....
....
....
....

The most beautiful Photo:

Name:

....

Message to Treasure:

The most beautiful Photo:

Name:

....

Message to Treasure:

....

....

....

....

....

....

....

....

....

The most beautiful Photo:

NAME:

....

MESSAGE TO TREASURE:

....
....
....
....
....
....
....
....
....

The most beautiful Photo:

Name:

....

Message to Treasure:

....

....

....

....

....

....

....

....

....

The most beautiful Photo:

Name:

....

Message to Treasure:

....
....
....
....
....
....
....
....
....

The most beautiful Photo:

NAME:

....

MESSAGE TO TREASURE:

....
....
....
....
....
....
....
....
....

The most beautiful Photo:

Name:

....

Message to Treasure:

....
....
....
....
....
....
....
....
....
....

The most beautiful Photo:

Name:

....

Message to Treasure:

....
....
....
....
....
....
....
....
....
....

The most beautiful Photo:

Name:

....

Message to Treasure:

....
....
....
....
....
....
....
....
....
....

The most beautiful Photo:

Name:

....

Message to Treasure:

....
....
....
....
....
....
....
....
....
....

The most beautiful Photo:

Name:

....

Message to Treasure:

....
....
....
....
....
....
....
....
....

The most beautiful Photo:

Name:

....

Message to Treasure:

....
....
....
....
....
....
....
....
....

The most beautiful Photo:

Name:

....

Message to Treasure:

The most beautiful Photo:

Name:

....

Message to Treasure:

....
....
....
....
....
....
....
....
....

The most beautiful Photo:

Name:

....

Message to Treasure:

....
....
....
....
....
....
....
....
....
....

The most beautiful Photo:

NAME:

....

MESSAGE TO TREASURE:

....
....
....
....
....
....
....
....
....

The most beautiful Photo:

Name:

....

Message to Treasure:

....
....
....
....
....
....
....
....
....

The most beautiful Photo:

Name:

....

Message to Treasure:

....
....
....
....
....
....
....
....
....
....

The most beautiful Photo:

NAME:

....

MESSAGE TO TREASURE:

....
....
....
....
....
....
....
....
....
....

The most beautiful Photo:

Name:

....

Message to Treasure:

....
....
....
....
....
....
....
....
....
....

The most beautiful Photo:

Name:

....

Message to Treasure:

....
....
....
....
....
....
....
....
....

The most beautiful Photo:

Name:

....

Message to Treasure:

....
....
....
....
....
....
....
....
....
....

The most beautiful Photo:

Name:

....

Message to Treasure:

....
....
....
....
....
....
....
....
....

The most beautiful Photo:

Name:

....

Message to Treasure:

....

....

....

....

....

....

....

....

....

The most beautiful Photo:

Name:

....

Message to Treasure:

....

....

....

....

....

....

....

....

....

The most beautiful Photo:

NAME:

....

MESSAGE TO TREASURE:

....
....
....
....
....
....
....
....
....

The most beautiful Photo:

NAME:

....

MESSAGE TO TREASURE:

....
....
....
....
....
....
....
....
....

Printed in France by Amazon
Brétigny-sur-Orge, FR

20494880R00047